JUST FOR FUN

SWING JAZZ UKULELE

12 CLASSICS FROM THE GOLDEN AGE OF JAZZ

Produced by
Alfred Music
P.O. Box 10003
Van Nuys, CA 91410-0003
alfred.com

Printed in USA.

ISBN-10: 1-4706-1439-1
ISBN-13: 978-1-4706-1439-3

Cover Photos
Central image models: Katrina Hruschka and Andrew Callahan / Photographer: Brian Immke, www.adeptstudios.com
3 Cherry uke: courtesy of C.F. Martin & Co • Moon: courtesy of The Library of Congress
Gramophone: © istockphoto / Faruk Tasdemir • MP3 player: © istockphoto / tpopova
Oldtimer car: © Fedor Selivanov / Shutterstock.com • Handstand: © istockphoto / jhorrocks • Jumping woman: © istockphoto / Dan Wilton
Swing dancers: © RetroClipArt / Shutterstock.com • Sneakers: © istockphoto / ozgurdonmaz
Background: image copyright Elise Gravel, 2009, used under license from Shutterstock.com

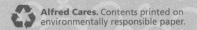

CONTENTS

AIN'T MISBEHAVIN'

Words by
ANDY RAZAF

Music by
THOMAS "FATS" WALLER
and HARRY BROOKS

Ain't Misbehavin' - 3 - 1

4

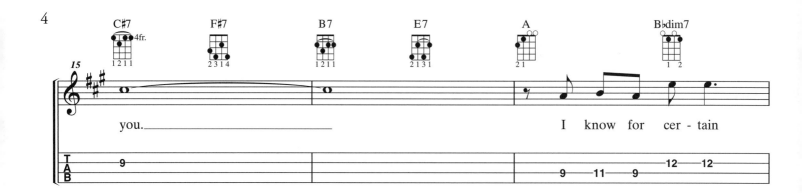

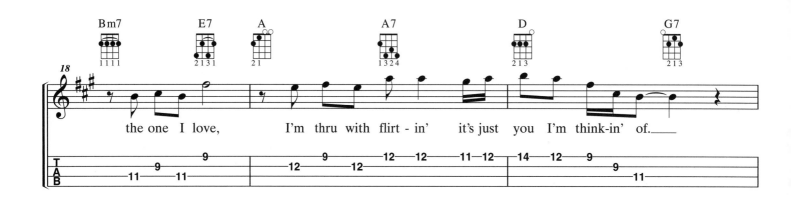

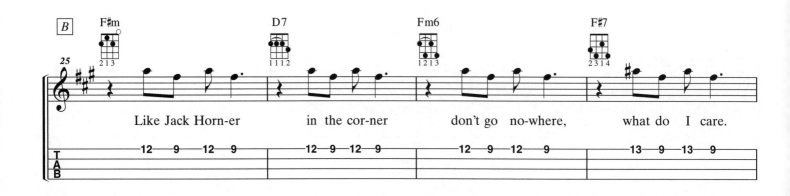

Ain't Misbehavin' - 3 - 2

BLUE MOON

Lyrics by
LORENZ HART

Music by
RICHARD RODGERS

Blue Moon - 4 - 1

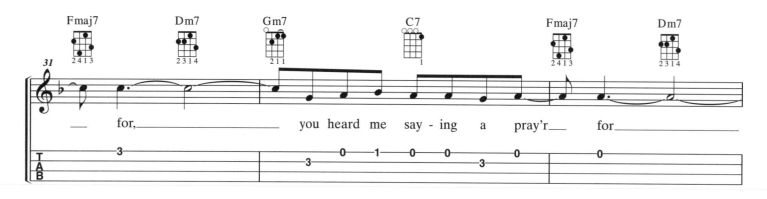

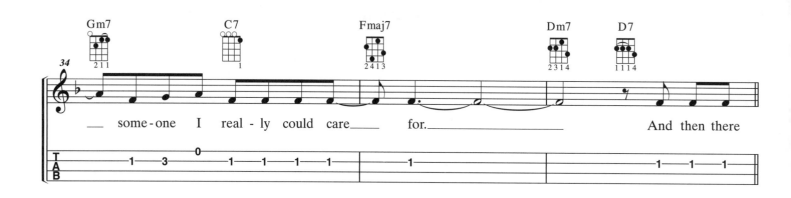

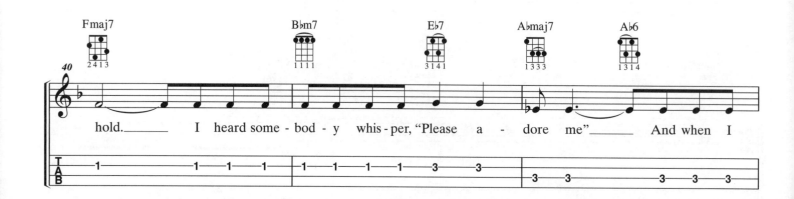

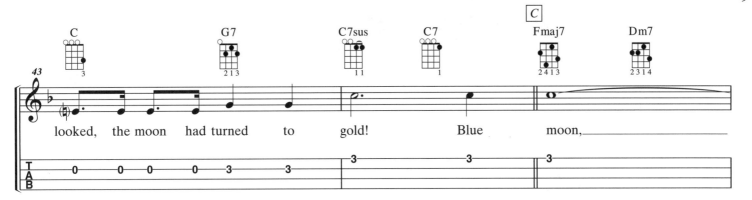

looked, the moon had turned to gold! Blue moon,_____

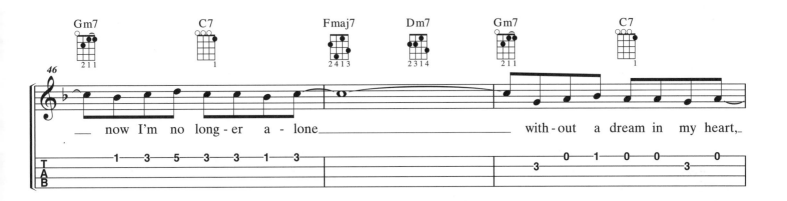

___ now I'm no long-er a-lone_____ with-out a dream in my heart,___

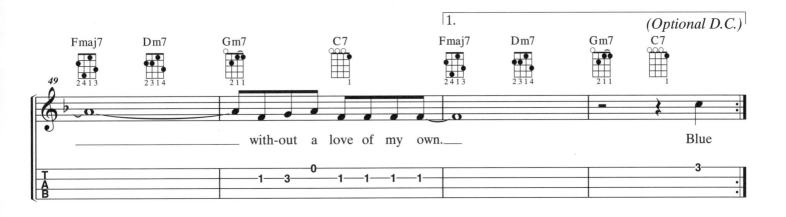

1. *(Optional D.C.)*

_____ with-out a love of my own.___ Blue

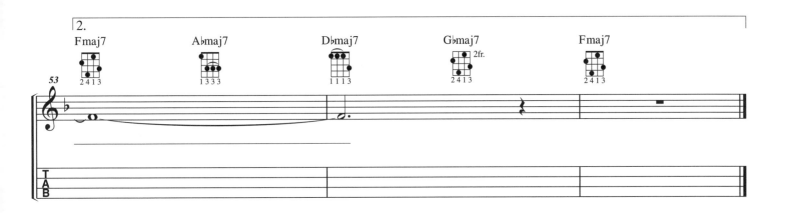

2.

BYE BYE BLACKBIRD

Words by
MORT DIXON

Music by
RAY HENDERSON

FIVE FOOT TWO, EYES OF BLUE

Lyrics by
SAM LEWIS and JOE YOUNG

Music by
RAY HENDERSON

Cont. in slashes

Five foot two, eyes of blue, but oh, what those five foot could do.__ Has

an - y - bod - y seen my gal?_____

Five Foot Two, Eyes of Blue - 3 - 1

I'LL SEE YOU IN MY DREAMS

Words by
GUS KAHN

Music by
ISHAM JONES

Medium swing

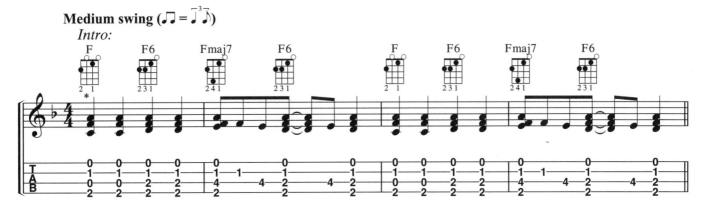

*Note: To keep the music notation easy to read, unison notes (same note/same octave)
are indicated only once in the notation but are shown clearly in the TAB and chord grids.

Verse:

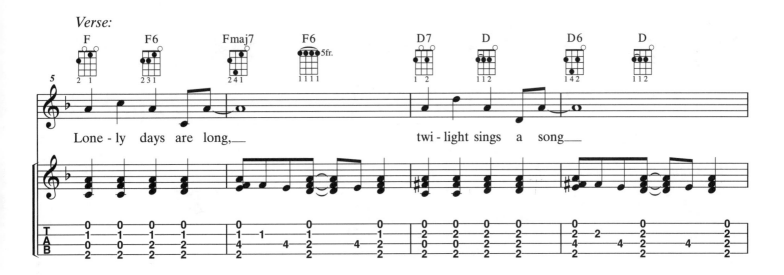

Lone - ly days are long,___ twi - light sings a song___

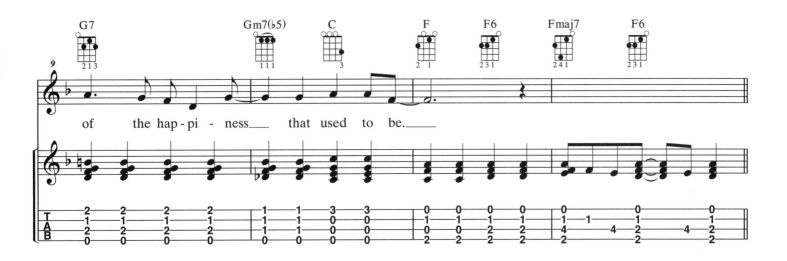

of the hap - pi - ness___ that used to be.___

I'll See You in My Dreams - 3 - 1

16

I'll See You in My Dreams - 3 - 2

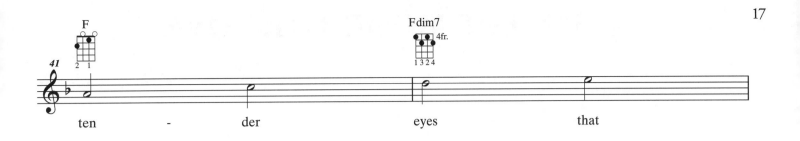

ten - der   eyes   that

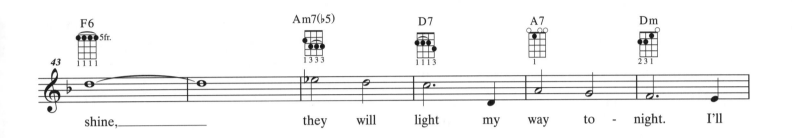

shine,_____   they will light my way to - night. I'll

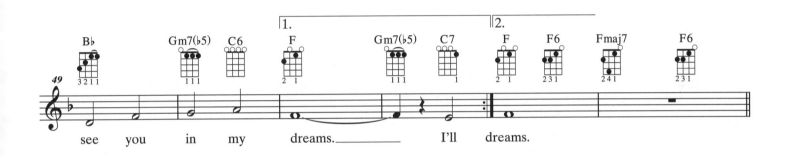

see you in my   dreams._____ I'll dreams.

Tag:

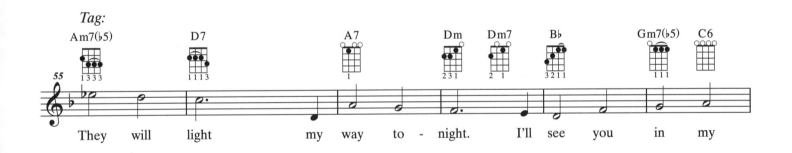

They will light   my way to - night.   I'll see you in my

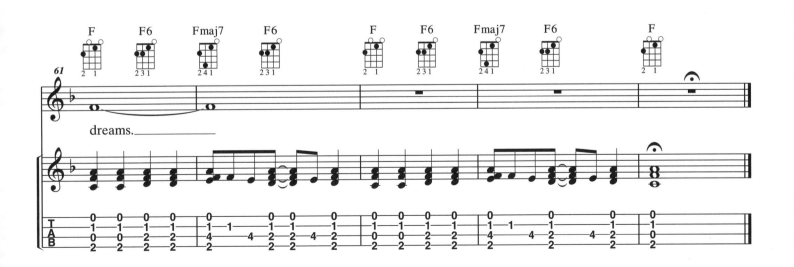

dreams._____

I'll See You in My Dreams - 3 - 3

I'M IN THE MOOD FOR LOVE

Words and Music by
JIMMY McHUGH and DOROTHY FIELDS

I'm in the mood for love, sim-ply be-cause you're near me.

Fun-ny, but when you're near me, I'm in the mood for love.

Heav-en is in your eyes, bright as the stars we're un-der.

Oh! Is it an-y won-der? I'm in the mood for love.

I'm in the Mood for Love - 2 - 1

I'm in the Mood for Love - 2 - 2

IT DON'T MEAN A THING
(If It Ain't Got That Swing)

Words by
IRVING MILLS

Music by
DUKE ELLINGTON

It Don't Mean a Thing (If It Ain't Got That Swing) - 2 - 1

MAKIN' WHOOPEE

Lyrics by
GUS KAHN

Music by
WALTER DONALDSON

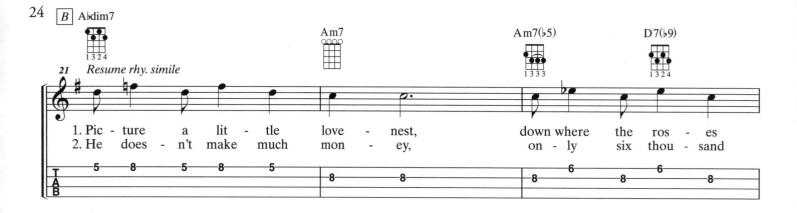

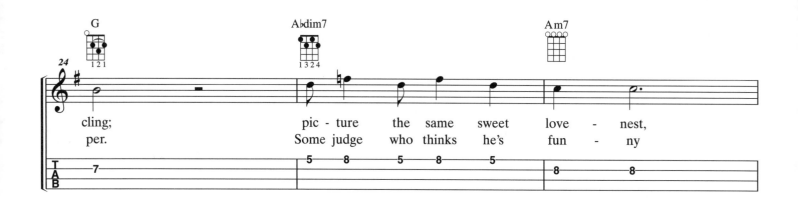

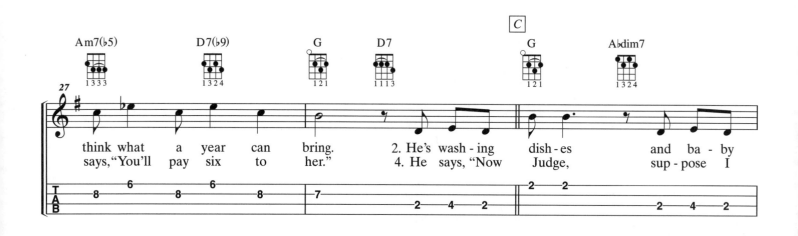

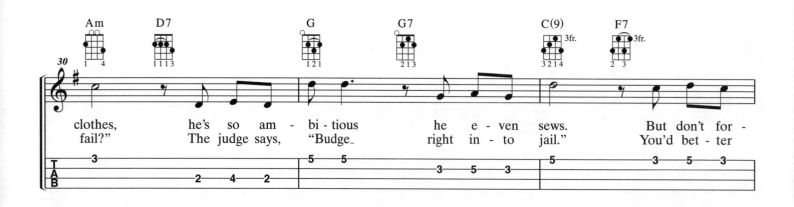

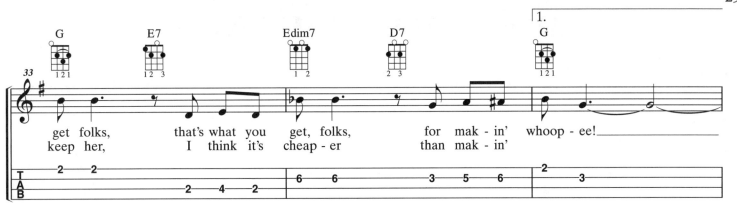

get folks, that's what you get, folks, for mak - in' whoop - ee!
keep her, I think it's cheap - er than mak - in'

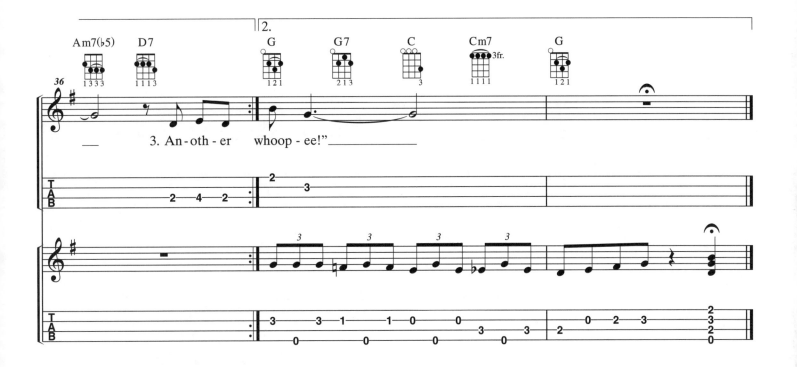

3. An - oth - er whoop - ee!"

MORE THAN YOU KNOW

Words by
WILLIAM ROSE and **EDWARD ELISCU**

Music by
VINCENT YOUMANS

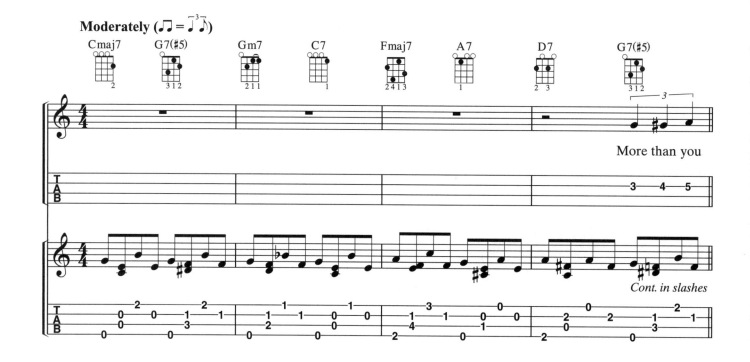

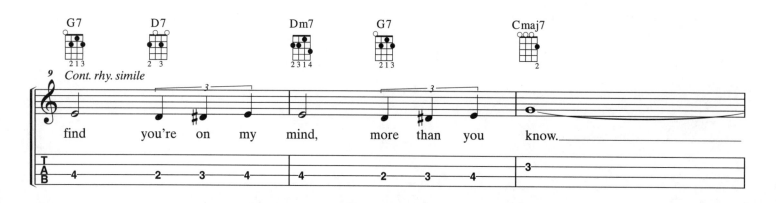

More Than You Know - 3 - 1

out it.　　　　　　　Oh, how I'd cry,　　oh, how I'd

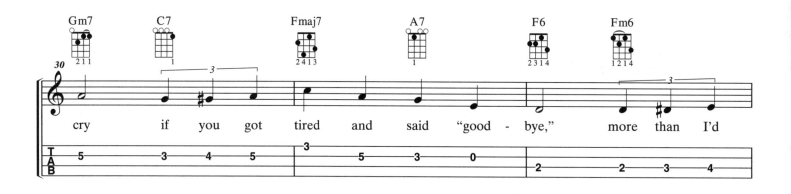

cry　　if you got tired and said "good - bye,"　　more than I'd

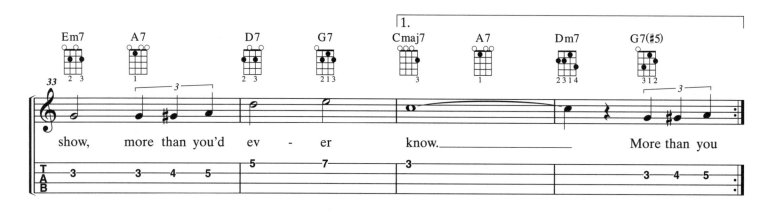

show, more than you'd ev - er know._____　　　　　More than you

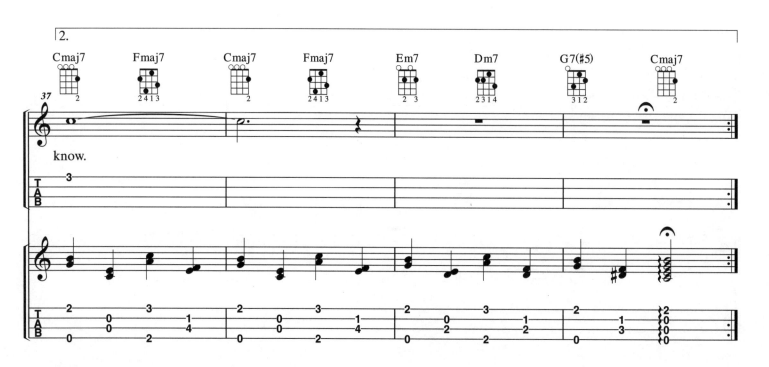

know.

SINGIN' IN THE RAIN

Lyric by
ARTHUR FREED

Music by
NACIO HERB BROWN

Singin' in the Rain - 3 - 1

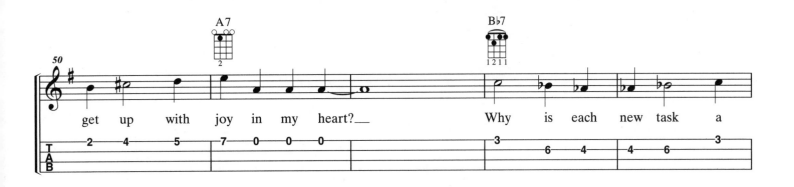

D.S. 𝄋 al Coda

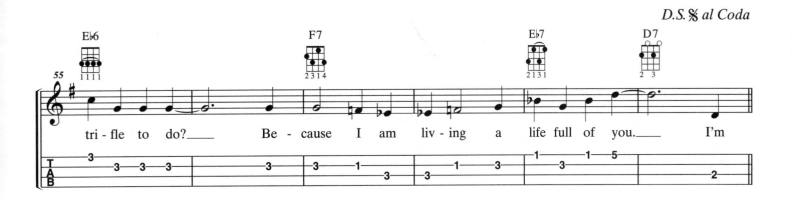

STARS FELL ON ALABAMA

Lyric by
MITCHELL PARISH

Music by
FRANK PERKINS

Stars Fell on Alabama - 3 - 1

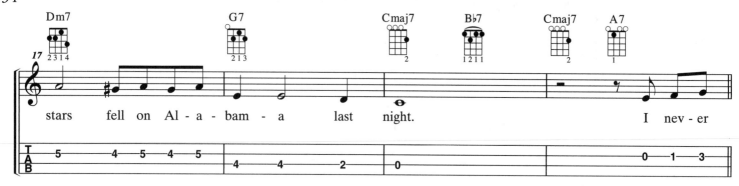

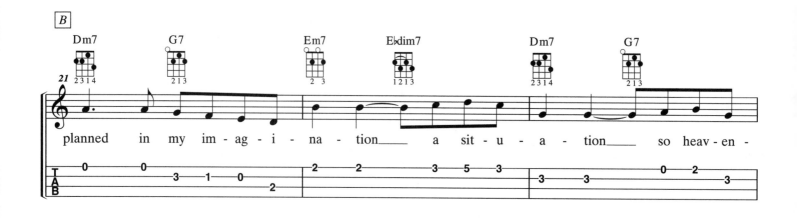

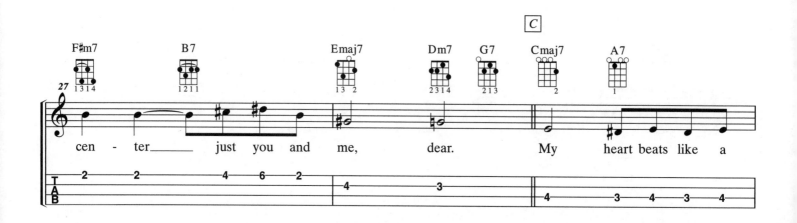

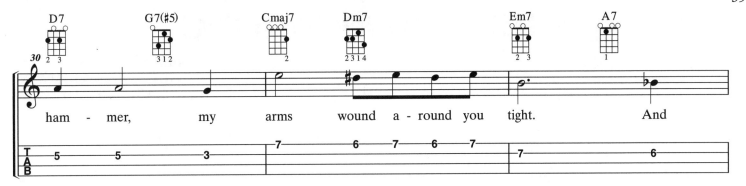

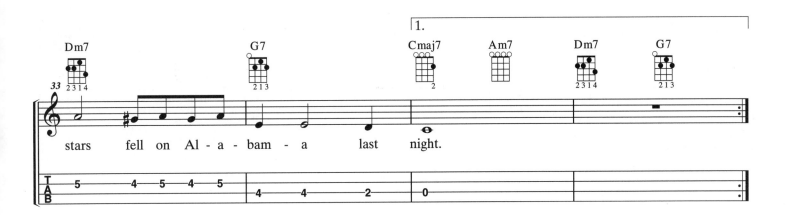

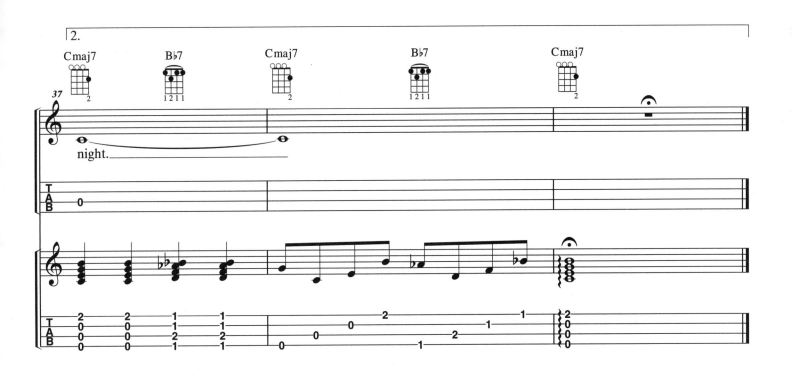

Stars Fell on Alabama - 3 - 3

WHEN YOU'RE SMILING

Words and Music by
MARK FISHER, JOE GOODWIN
and LARRY SHAY

When You're Smiling - 2 - 1

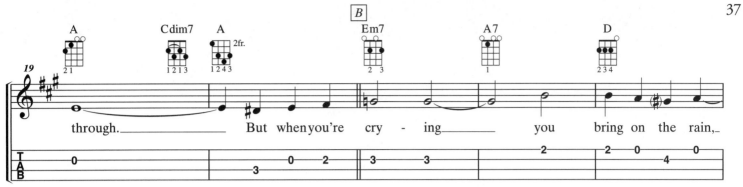

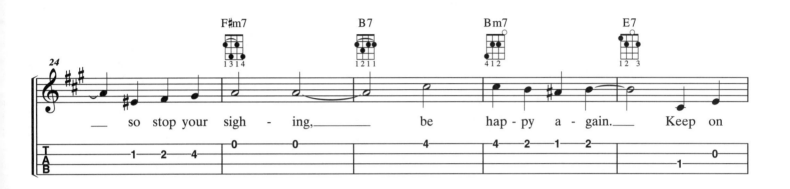

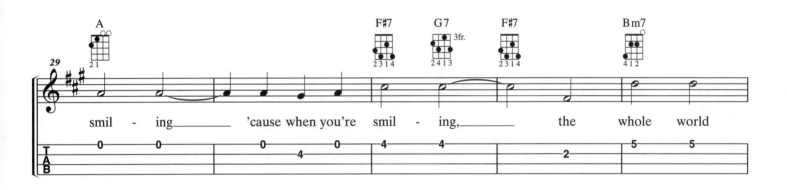

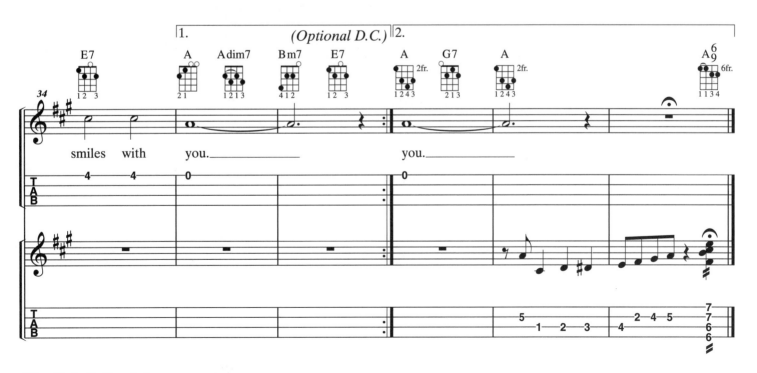

When You're Smiling - 2 - 2

UKULELE CHORD DICTIONARY

A CHORDS

A
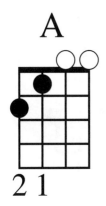
2 1

A
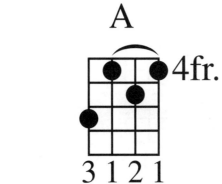
4fr.
3 1 2 1

Amaj7
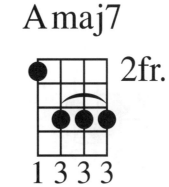
2fr.
1 3 3 3

A6
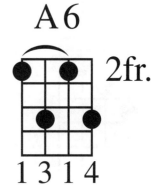
2fr.
1 3 1 4

Am
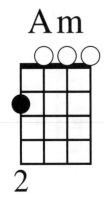
2

Am
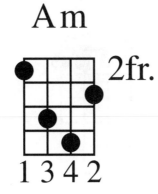
2fr.
1 3 4 2

Am7
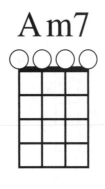

Am6
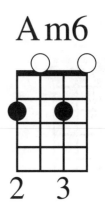
2 3

A7
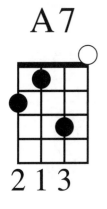
2 1 3

A7
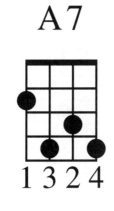
1 3 2 4

A9
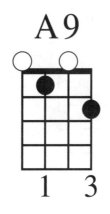
1 3

A13

1 2 3

Asus
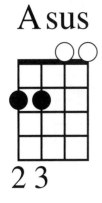
2 3

A7sus
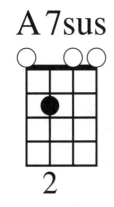
2

Adim7
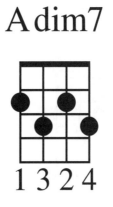
1 3 2 4

A+
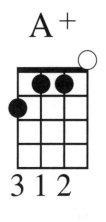
3 1 2

B♭ (A♯) CHORDS*

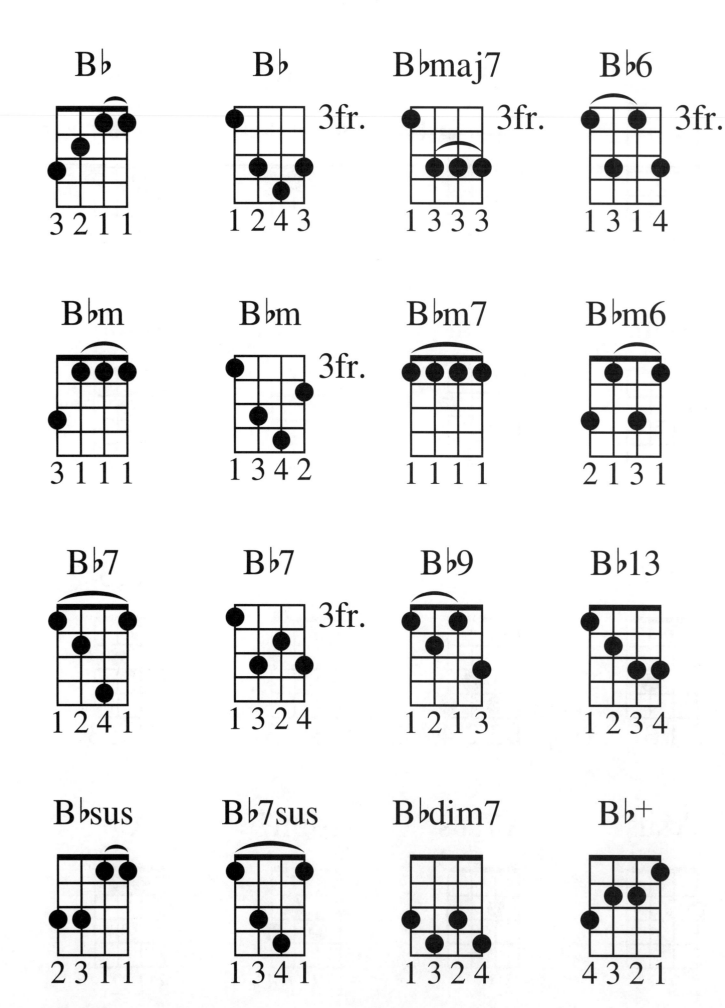

*B♭ and A♯ are two names for the same note.

B CHORDS

B
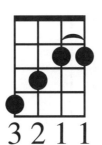
3 2 1 1

B
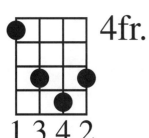
4fr.
1 3 4 2

Bmaj7
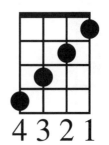
4 3 2 1

B6
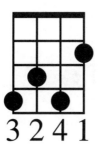
3 2 4 1

Bm
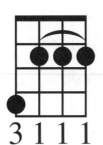
3 1 1 1

Bm
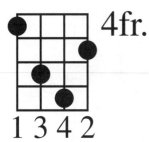
4fr.
1 3 4 2

Bm7
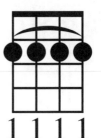
1 1 1 1

Bm6

2 1 3 1

B7

3 2 1

B7
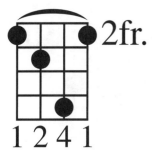
2fr.
1 2 4 1

B9
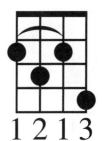
1 2 1 3

B13
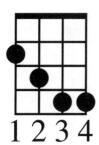
1 2 3 4

Bsus
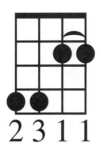
2 3 1 1

B7sus

1 3 1 1

Bdim7

1 3 2 4

B+
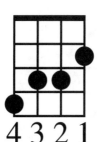
4 3 2 1

C CHORDS

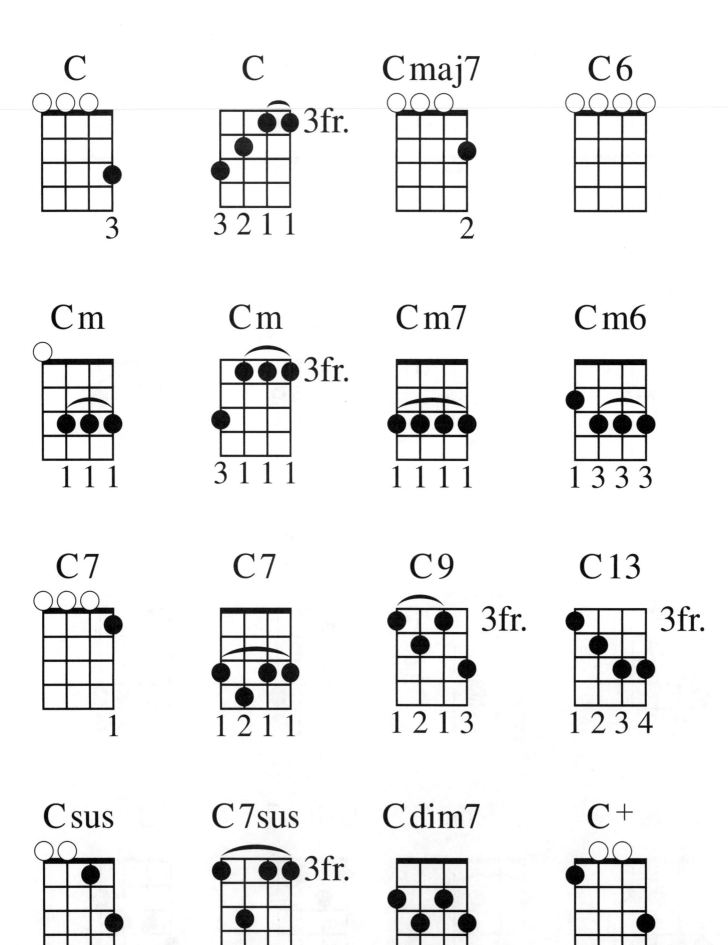

C♯ (D♭) CHORDS*

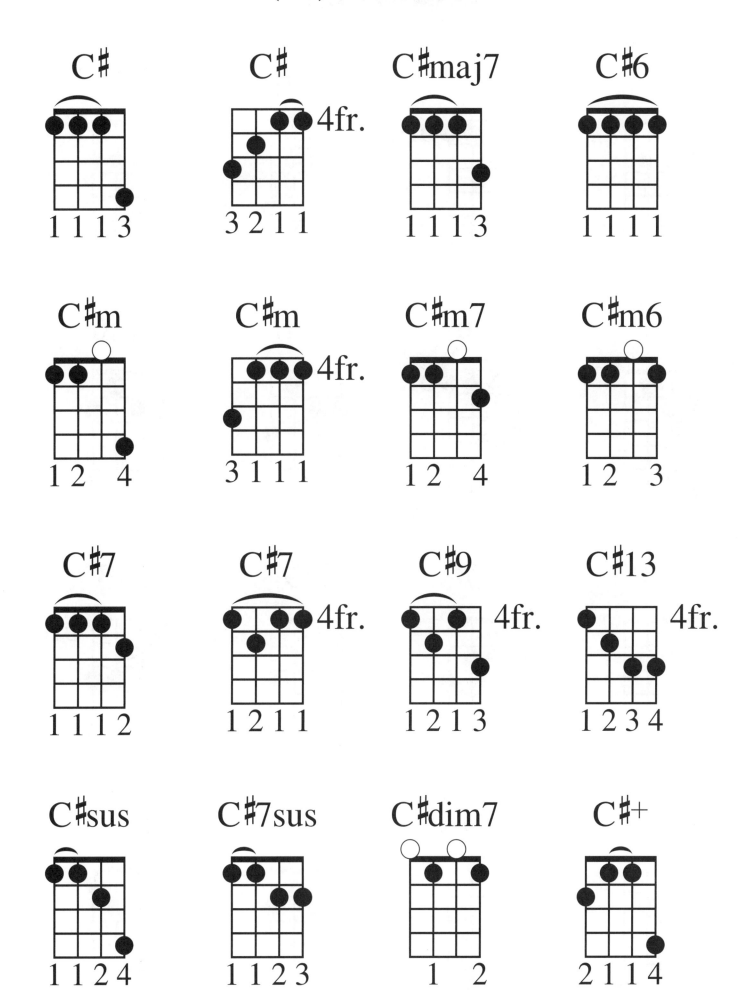

*C♯ and D♭ are two names for the same note.

D CHORDS

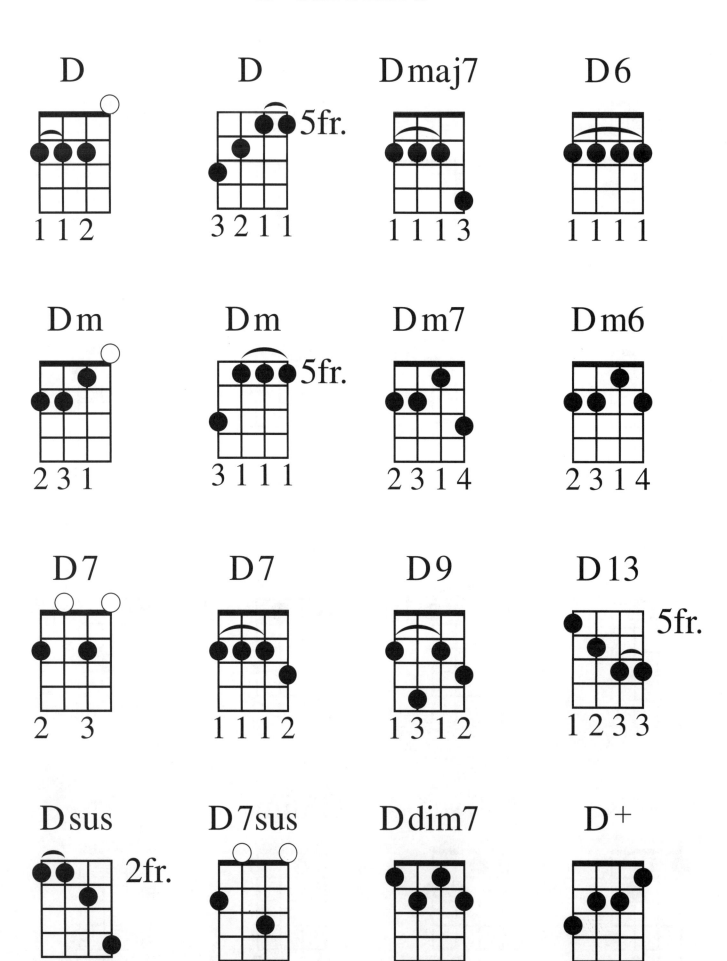

E♭ (D♯) CHORDS*

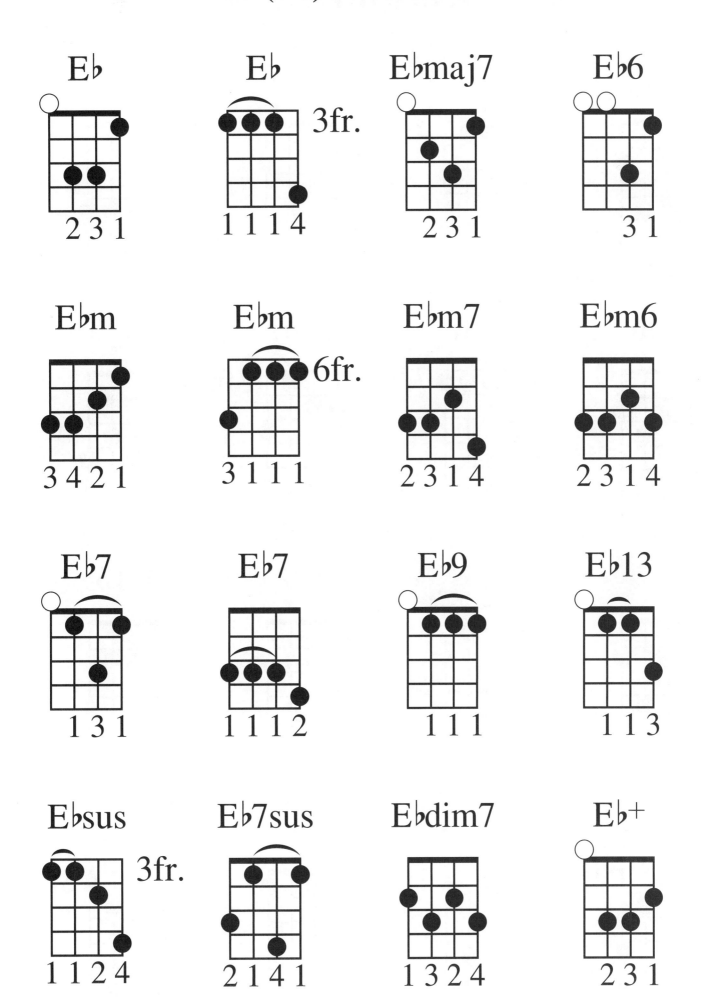

*E♭ and D♯ are two names for the same note.

E CHORDS

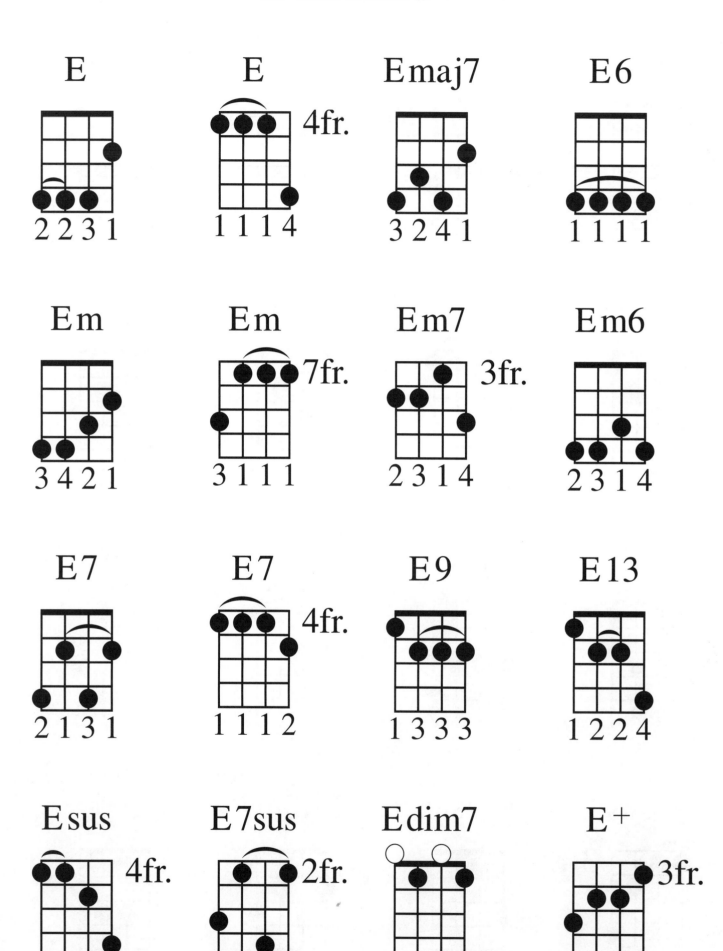

F CHORDS

F
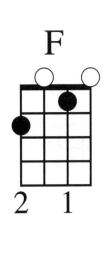
2   1

F
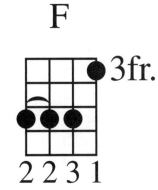
3fr.
2 2 3 1

Fmaj7

2

F6
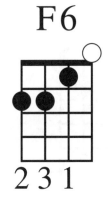
2 3 1

Fm
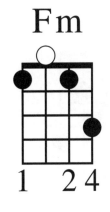
1 2 4

Fm
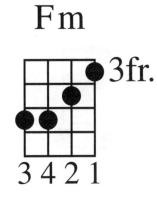
3fr.
3 4 2 1

Fm7
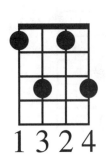
1 3 2 4

Fm6

1 3 2 4

F7
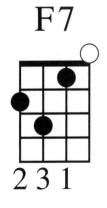
2 3 1

F7
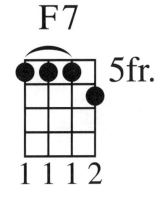
5fr.
1 1 1 2

F9
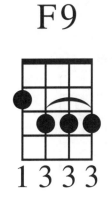
1 3 3 3

F13
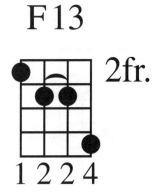
2fr.
1 2 2 4

Fsus
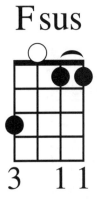
3 1 1

F7sus
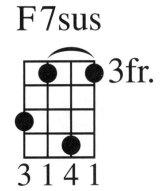
3fr.
3 1 4 1

Fdim7
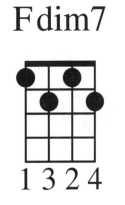
1 3 2 4

F+
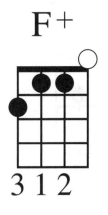
3 1 2

F♯ (G♭) CHORDS*

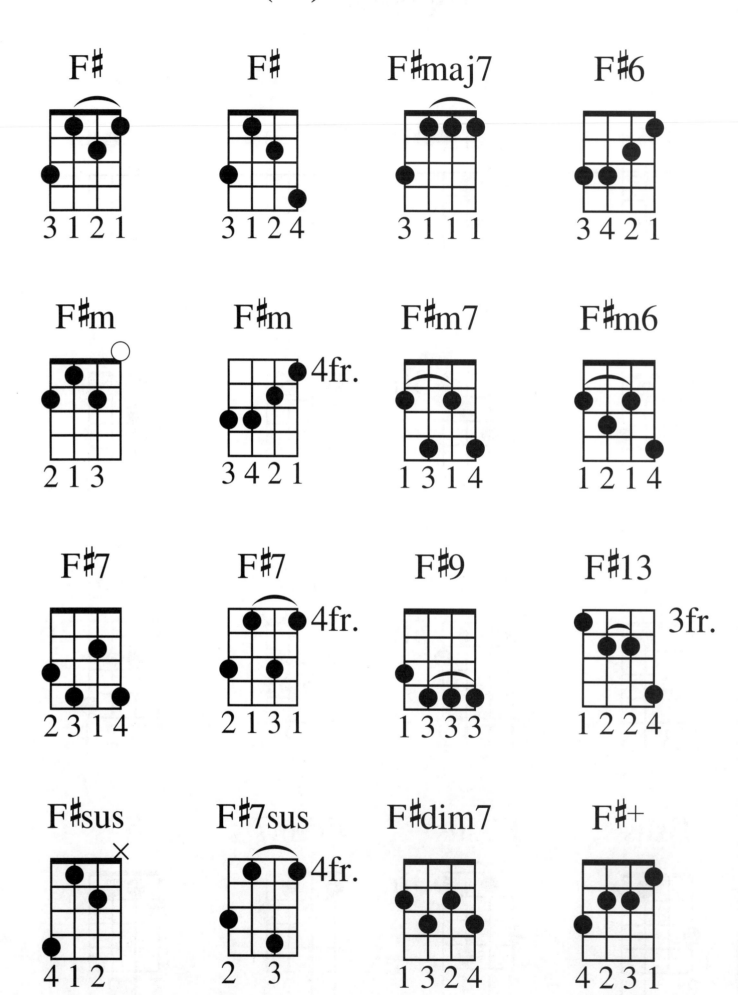

*F♯ and G♭ are two names for the same note.

G CHORDS

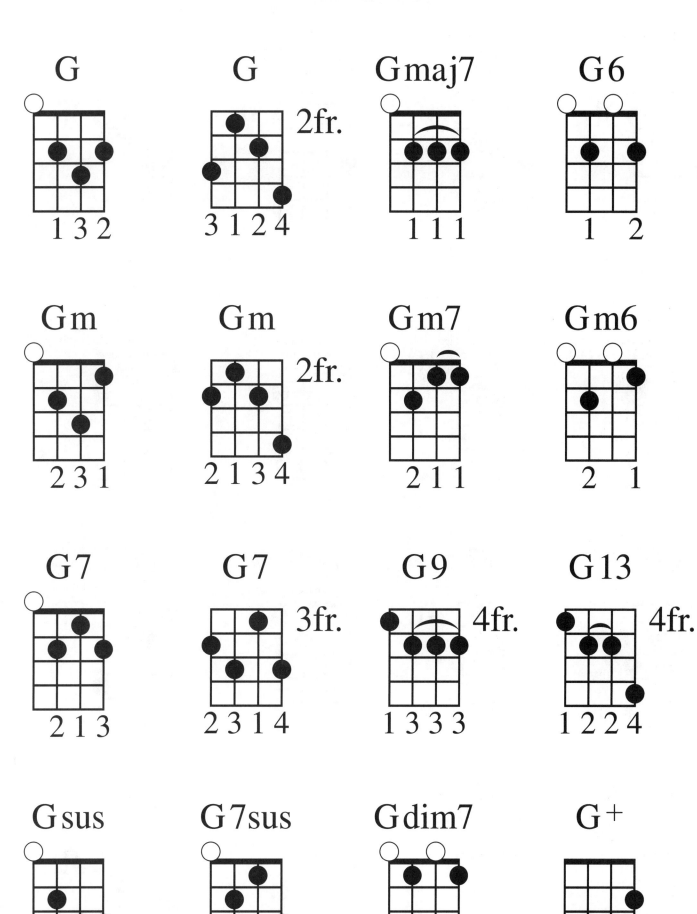

A♭ (G♯) CHORDS

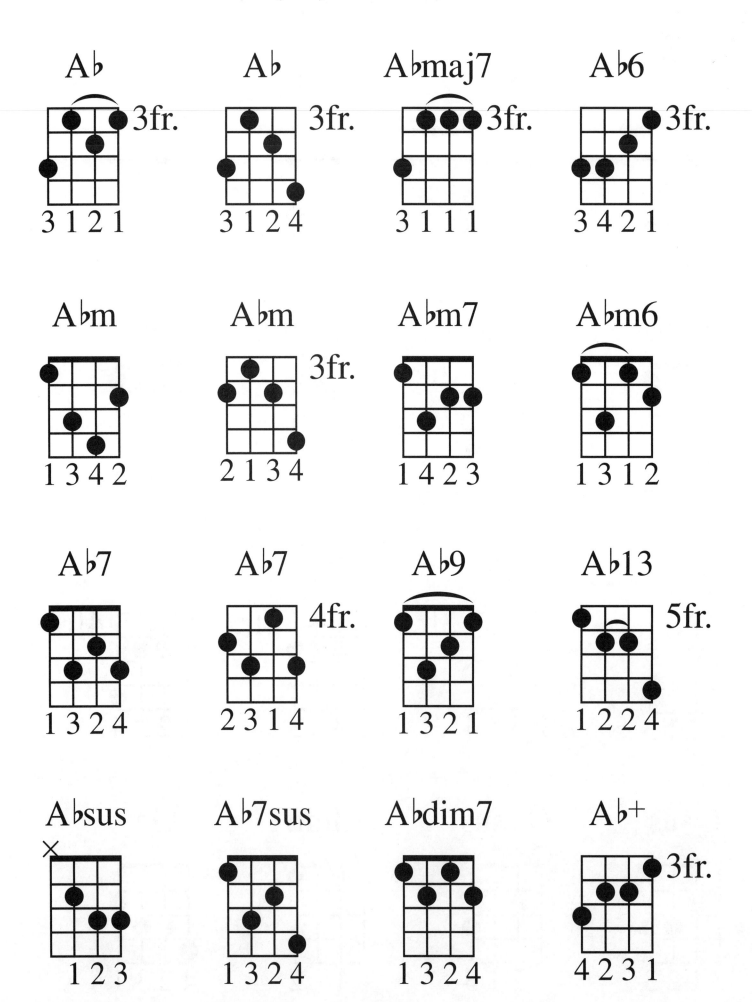

TABLATURE EXPLANATION
TAB illustrates the four strings of the ukulele.
Notes and chords are indicated by the placement of fret numbers on each string.

Standard ukulele tuning for soprano, concert, and tenor models is G–C–E–A with the fourth string tuned a whole step lower than the open 1st string.

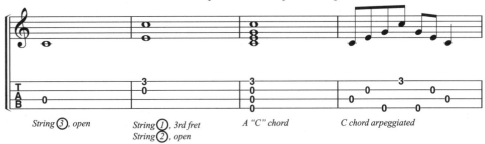

String ③, open   *String ①, 3rd fret*   *A "C" chord*   *C chord arpeggiated*
String ②, open

Alternate Tuning:
Some players (including Israel "Iz" Kamakawiwoʻole) tune their fourth string down one octave from standard ukulele (similar to the first four strings of a guitar with a capo on the 5th fret).

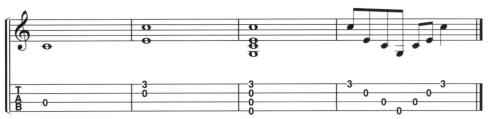

ARTICULATIONS

Hammer On:
Play the lower note, then "hammer" your finger to the higher note. Only the first note is plucked.

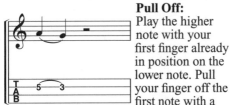

Pull Off:
Play the higher note with your first finger already in position on the lower note. Pull your finger off the first note with a strong downward motion that plucks the string—sounding the lower note.

Legato Slide:
Play the first note and, keeping pressure applied on the string, slide up to the second note. The diagonal line shows that it is a slide and not a hammer-on or a pull-off.

Palm Mute:
The notes are muted (muffled) by placing the palm of the pick hand lightly on the strings, just in front of the bridge.

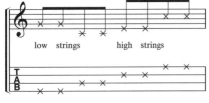

Muted Strings:
A percussive sound is produced by striking the strings while laying the fret hand across them.

HARMONICS

Natural Harmonic:
A finger of the fret hand lightly touches the string at the note indicated in the TAB and is plucked by the pick producing a bell-like sound called a harmonic.

RHYTHM SLASHES

Strum Marks/ Rhythm Slashes:
Strum with the indicated rhythm pattern. Strum marks can be located above the staff or within the staff.

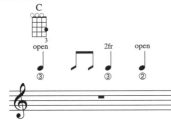

Single Notes with Rhythm Slashes:
Sometimes single notes are incorporated into a strum pattern. The circled number below is the string and the fret number is above.

PICK DIRECTION

Downstrokes and Upstrokes:
The downstroke is indicated with this symbol ⊓ and the upstroke is indicated with this ∨.

BENDING NOTES

Slight Bend/ Quarter-Tone Bend:
Play the note and bend string sharp.

Half Step:
Play the note and bend string one half step (one fret).